Ashes of The Past

Poetry Within My Notebook

By Sierra Dean

ISBN-13: 978-0-9975042-3-1

Library of Congress Control Number 2018907695

Editing by Stella Joy

Book Design and Front Cover Image by Twon Jee

Printed and bound in the United States of America
First Printing August 2018

Published by Dean Diaries LLC
PO 23033
St. Louis, MO 63156

www.deandiaries.com

Table of Contents

"The next time you sense a strong emotion, take some time to put a finger on exactly what you're feeling. Get quiet, turn inward, and just listen..."

~Lisa Nichols

Consideration

About you

So, I'm sitting here wondering how I want to think of you today.

You want me to explain how I think of you.

But where can I start, where can I end?

Our relationship is endless, and I'm not sure how it ever began.

There was only one time you hurt me but it brought us closer.

After that point, it made me realize what our friendship was all about.

I'm able to come to you and talk to you about anything.

I know that you will never judge me and let me know how you are feeling.

Even if I don't agree with you.

There are times I don't.

You are a wonderful friend.

Kind of like a sister.

I'm glad that we were able to become as much as we are.

I never want to lose what we have.

No matter how many days we spend apart.

We can always come back together and catch up.

Even though you are a crazy individual.

I still love everything about you and never would want anyone else to take your place.

So, I hope that this will never end.

Friendship is priceless.

For A Reason

God brings people in your life for a reason.

There's always a time and a season for everything and everyone.

Just never try to take advantage, when you're given one.

There's always a need for something in life.

You just can't get there without another person.

Once this has been realized, everything will be a lot easier to deal with.

You will learn how to understand.

Love everyone for who they are.

Some people come into your life just to take you down.

There's always someone to jump in to bring you right back up.

Nothing will always be perfect in life.

Know that everyone is not brought into your life for a lifetime.

Keep loving yourself and your neighbor.

Most importantly, love God.

God is the one making everything happen.

Nobody can get to a great place in life without going through the bad.

Everyone is brought into your life for a reason and a season.

Silence

I hear your silent cry.

I hear your loud laughter.

I know there is pain inside from the morning after.

The pain that may never go away.

Yet you hide behind the smile.

You wonder why it stays.

Stays with you day and night.

Never leaving your side.

This is you, but yet you still fight.

Fight for what was then and still is now.

Move on from the past.

You just don't know how.

You just keep smiling.

Hiding behind that mask.

Someone will come up to you to ask, "Why are you so happy?"

Then you say, "That's just me."

Yet, deep down inside, you know that you are not complete.

Calling out to be free.

From the pain that hides beneath.

Why don't you just say what it is and let it be?

Yet, you're hiding behind that smile, refusing to see what is skin deep.

What happened?

I'm chasing a dream.

I'm chasing reality.

I'm just sitting here wondering how it would turn out.

I look at the past and see I had a future.

But then, I stopped and wondered what happened to you.

I'm off track.

Where did my head go?

On the wrong road a long time ago?

I can't figure this out, but I'm getting too bored.

I better do something before too much information is stored.

In this brain of mine, it wonders too far.

To this other world where I think I'm a star.

Sitting on a cloud away from all of the commotion.

Wonder what would happen if my mind just stayed open.

Wishing you were the same

What used to be was us.

What used to be was someone that I could talk to.

Now you are the enemy.

My own kind.

How could you turn on me like this?

I make up with outsiders.

But can't seem to make up with you.

How can we just be true again?

Without an argument.

My energy is gone.

There is none left.

The respect is gone.

Without regret.

I have this feeling inside of me that wants to say something.

Then, I don't want to say anything.

You make me feel like it's my fault.

You act like a kid.

Start owning your own faults.

Be someone to look up to.

You used to be that person.

Now you are nothing to me.

Will things ever be the same as the old days?

Wait, these aren't the old days.

I'm so frustrated because I'm missing something that I used to have.

That is, you.

Someone that didn't act brand new.

Someone I knew that I could talk to.

Now you are nothing to me.

I'm not supposed to feel this way.

Then, how can I put my all into someone that is selfish?

Selfish and only cares about their feelings.

What about mine?

Do you even care?

Have you ever?

Just hear me out because I want things to get better.

Things will never be the same.

It seems this way.

I'm hoping that the sun will shine down on you again someday.

Confusion

Feeling helpless

Nobody knew what it felt like for me to feel alone.

Nobody knew what it felt like to need a place to call home.

Home not being in a literal sense.

But just needing a place to feel comfort and care.

Nobody was there when I needed them.

I was afraid.

I was alone.

There was not one person there when I closed my eyes.

Hoping that my last breath would come.

Once it did, I saw everything happen before my very eyes.

What if it happened, how would people feel?

What would they think of me?

Would they wonder why I didn't call them when I needed comforting?

But everyone should've known how I was feeling.

I guess I was just being selfish, since I felt no feelings.

No feelings at the time about what was going on.

I should have known that I would be okay.

Then I found myself praying.

Praying about something that I knew would change.

But I was ready for the change to happen at that moment.

How did I make it there?

Why did I have no fear?

No fear of what was going on?

The feelings I had were so cold.

I cry

Nobody will ever know the pain I feel inside.

The pain that begins to cry.

The thunder of the storm that surrounds my brain.

I cry.

I cry intensely when I think about the pain.

The pain that I felt that day and that night.

I cry.

Will it ever go away?

When will I see my rainbow?

You took my sunshine away.

You made me feel nothing but darkness.

I cry.

When my heart begins to hurt.

I lay down and cry.

Cry for reasons beyond me.

This is just too much for me.

With no one to call when my body is suffering.

I cry.

Feeling the pain of the past, present and future.

I cry.

I need to leave

Why am I here?

Where should I be?

These are questions that are burning deep inside of me.

My motivation is sinking like my workload is quicksand, that I keep stepping into by mistake and can't seem to get out.

I asked for so much guidance and strength to get through the day or maybe even just a moment.

I'm not meant to be here.

Why don't I just leave?

Because I need to survive?

That moment in life where I know what I want, and I know where my happiness lies.

It's not here.

Why do I do this to myself every day?

Spend most of my valuable time somewhere that I don't even want to be.

I'm not happy.

How can I find happiness again?

There and Back

Have you ever loved someone more than you loved yourself?

Every day, that's all you were able to think of.

Have you ever been in a place where you never knew, where you would end up?

Have you ever been lost, not knowing how you would make it back?

Have you ever listened to your heartbeat and wondered when it would stop?

Have you ever been there?

Have you ever been so lonely, that you didn't know if anyone would ever come to keep you company?

Have you ever had so many thoughts in your head, not knowing which one to follow?

Have you ever?

Have you ever wondered if you loved, since you were never kept in that place?

Have you ever?

Have you ever wondered why nothing ever goes your way, wondering if you would make it?

Have you?

Have you ever been down that road not knowing which way to turn?

Have you ever been there?

Empty Receivers

I remember sitting there, not knowing who to call.

Was there anyone ever there to listen?

Was I ever heard?

Did people even think of me and wonder how I felt?

Did I have someone to call?

Did I ever have something to say?

Maybe not.

Who could make me laugh, for me to feel better?

Would anyone even care?

Who could I call?

Everyone is always too busy.

Maybe I was.

Would they even listen?

Would they even care?

Who can I call?

I stare at the phone without a number to dial.

Why won't they listen?

I'm trying to let them in.

I'm scared that they won't understand.

Please let me know who I can call.

I'm still staring at the phone, but nobody is calling.

Maybe my phone is off.

Happy*

Sometimes I cry, thinking about the things that I could have and what I don't.

I wish that people were able to understand me.

It seems as if I smile to make things much better.

I know they will never be.

How can I ever express the way I feel, without being sad or worried?

What should I do?

I'm not sure what to do.

Why do I cry?

Is it to make me feel better?

Is it to help me get over my fears and wants?

It seems as if the crying never helps.

The tears roll down until they're gone.

I look to the left and the right.

Nobody is there to help wipe them away.

How do I cope?

I'm not sure.

I try to make me happy, in the end, I'm not.

People may think I have a perfect life, but I don't.

Soul, Mind, Spirit, and Purpose

I'm running down this dark path at full speed, not knowing what is in front of me.

Wondering, if I should turn around because there may be light behind me.

But I don't see it; maybe it's far in the distance.

I may as well keep running because I've made it this far.

There's no turning back.

Now, I'm at this road.

Oh no, there's three.

Three too many.

I no longer see what's in front of me.

Then I realize my soul is one path.

I feel so weak.

I feel so confused, but no one will understand me.

My soul is so cold at times.

Should I choose that road because my soul has not chosen me?

Leaving me weary and weak.

I'm just not ready.

Now I realize my mind is staring right at me.

I can't seem to stay focused.

My mind is constantly racing.

I try to take control, but I can't.

For a moment, it's subtle.

Then it's back overflowing.

My spirit is empty.

Who or what should I turn to?

With nothing to believe, my spirit feels empty.

Please feel me up.

My spirit needs healing.

There's nothing to turn to but my purpose.

I know what I want yet, I'm still searching for what I need.

Time to make my way towards the trees because my purpose will never fail me.

Dreary

I felt as if I had no soul.

I felt as if there was a hole.

A hole deep inside of me. It needed to be filled.

Because there was no way I should feel the way I felt.

But I laid there, I prayed.

I heard my heart beating in my head.

I knew it was about to be over.

The Lord spoke to me and reminded me that I was a soldier.

I was able to get through this because I was able to take this pain.

Now I feel like a stronger person, and there is so much that I've gained.

I never thought I would have feelings of emptiness.

Now I know what it feels like to be born again.

The pain that made me go insane.

Help me to refrain from the strain, of a helpless soul.

That one that needed to be consoled.

Thoughts of leaving

Some people are meant to be here, but I'm not.

I was meant to be here years ago but now my time has expired.

How can I just leave a place that I've been for years?

I grew up in this space.

This space helped me to grow into the person I am today.

Why am I holding on to this place that no longer fulfills me?

No longer makes me whole?

No longer loves me?

Now I'm just finding myself content in this space.

In this space, I no longer belong.

I'm becoming afraid to leave, and anxiety is flowing everywhere through me.

I'm struggling with my thoughts.

I'm struggling with my peace.

This place made me who I am.

Well, at least helped me to understand who I am.

I find myself crying at night when I'm alone in my thoughts.

The thoughts in my head make it so hard for me to even go to bed.

Why am I living in this complacency?

This is not where I want to be.

My thoughts are starting to overtake me.

I'm living outside of my body.

I know what I need to do and what is in me.

I just can't force myself to leave.

Did I forget all of the self-worth that I hold?

Am I putting my self-love behind me?

Why do I let somebody else's dream dictate my wholeness?

I can create my own.

This is my world and mine alone.

I need to just leave and get out of this complacency.

Everyone told me it would be hard, but I never knew it would be like this.

I just wasn't ready.

From crying in my head to crying out loud.

I know that this will be over soon.

That day when I leave.

Relationships

Every time I think of you

Every time I think of you, I think of your soft touch.

That moment when everything, seems to be gone.

How is it that you make me feel like this?

How could this be real?

"It's just too good to be true" as Lauryn Hill said, "I can't keep my eyes off of you".

You make me feel good in every way.

There are so many things I could say, but I want you to know, that I feel this way.

Why can't you see?

I'm sure that this is not what you want.

This was not in the plan, but I just wonder if you ever thought, of being my man.

Every time I think of you, a sensation flow through me.

Maybe it's just going too deep.

I really can't figure out where this is all coming from. I just feel like sometimes, I need to run.

Away from my feelings.

Away from the future.

Away from you because I'm sure this won't last.

Why should I feel this way, just to run away?

It's just me but there's still more, I could say.

Every time I think of you, I want it more because I love when you make me feel good to the core.

It just feels so good from every touch.

I should flee because I'm starting to think of you too much.

I don't love you

Why is it that you love me so much, even when I make you feel this way?

I don't show you any love and affection, yet you still want to hear from me.

Calling my phone every day, just to check up on me to make sure, I'm doing okay.

How is it that I make you feel this way?

Why do you put all of your energy in me, to love you?

Isn't it obvious to you that I never will?

Love doesn't grow just because you want it to.

Love usually grows when you're not trying to.

I don't want to hurt you or even come on to you.

I don't even want to walk away because I know that I'm the only one, that you hold on to.

But then, I don't want to come on to you because I know it's not something that I want to do.

You love me so much, but I don't love you.

I just need to let you go now and I'm still trying to.

I want you

Well, I find myself sitting here every day, thinking of you.

Which I know that I don't need to do.

You're so content with the way your life is right now.

It comes down to the fact that it will all be up to you.

Where will this go?

When will this end?

Will we end up the best of friends?

I want to feel you so bad, but I can't tell you.

That I would love to wake up to your smell.

I want to feel your lips next to mine.

Your heart will feel just fine.

When I gaze into your eyes, I tend to look too far.

Sometimes, it feels like I'm wishing on a star.

Wanting you to feel the way I do.

I just want it to be true.

Don't lie to me, just make me feel brand new.

I feel like if I were to fall in love with you, I will feel brand new.

I'm starting to love so much about your character and the things
that you do.

I don't feel this way often, but I just need to face the reality that what I feel is true.

Should I tell you?

I've thought this to myself.

Maybe because I don't want to feel the rejection.

Knowing that you don't want me, the way I want you.

I want to be with you.

Love in your hands

Instead of loving you.

I love me too much, but I've just never seen such.

How can a person be so loving? Yet not caring.

Caring for others' feelings, just seems so unbarring.

The love that I'm still trying to find, is yet something that I still want as mine.

Do I need you I ask?

My mind says no, but I know that I do.

I need you to love me as much as I love myself.

Why would I put my love in the hands of another person, when I know how to do it better?

There comes silence when I know I need you.

Hold me, caress me, and comfort me.

Why can't I have this?

Putting my love in your hands, will be so hard to do.

How will I know that the love is true?

What I would do to give you, that power to love me.

Will I then, define everything that you do?

Will you be able to satisfy me? Which I know that I can already do.

Well, I'm in love with me, and I don't want to give my heart to you.

You may abuse the fact that my love is true.

Kindhearted and knows what I want.

How can I give my heart and love to you?

Meeting someone new

Getting to know you.

You open my eyes to so much more.

You were able to let me in, without hesitation.

You helped me to learn that everyone is not the same.

Everyone doesn't always go insane.

Insane from the pain.

I came in this with a closed mind.

Not knowing, if this would even last.

I gave myself about a month or so.

Then it will be over.

But you tricked me.

There was so much more that you had to offer.

Intelligence, dedication, inspiration, and a beautiful friendship.

You helped me learn to trust again.

I stopped trying to find that friend.

Someone like you that came to me so true.

I didn't expect this.

I'm not sure how and why this is happening.

I know that you are very admiring.

I admire you a lot.

I wouldn't want you to change.

You helped me through my pain.

Pain that I'm not willing to share with you right now.

It's not completely gone.

I'm just glad that I was willing to stay.

Should I tell you I love you?

Wanting to let you know that I love you, is killing me so slowly inside.

The anxiety of wondering if you feel the same or thinking this, has even come to mind.

Your mind at least, because I know this was not meant to be.

Maybe when I say this, you will feel the same.

If I wait too long, I may drive myself insane.

I should take the time for you to tell me first.

Then it may be too late because someone else may come in and take it.

Take that heart of yours that I feel so deep.

But then, I'm still afraid that you may run quickly.

Quickly away from me.

Because you don't want this to be.

The anxiety of this all is slowly killing me.

I just need to say how I feel because how I feel is real.

I just can't keep holding on to this, so what's the deal?

Thoughts of a victim in denial

There was a moment when I was happy with you.

There was a moment when I wanted to spend the rest of my life with you.

I started to feel complete and whole all around.

I didn't care what anyone would say about you.

I didn't care if anyone liked you, but I didn't care if anyone liked me either.

You always said that you would make me happy no matter what it took.

Then I told you that I would never leave you, I knew that I was hooked.

I was hooked on the love that I never had.

I was hooked on just being with someone.

I used to always see other couples and become jealous, I wanted what they had.

Now I question what I used to want but then, I wonder if what I had was even bad.

It was great in the beginning, well, at least to me.

Everyone was able to see through something I could not see.

Then I began to question.

Why am I letting someone else dictate my happiness?

I knew that what I felt was real.

I knew that I was happy.

Why didn't people just accept that fact and let me be?

Why am I feeling this way?

Every time I look at you, I wonder what tomorrow will bring.

I wonder if you will leave me after you get everything you want from me.

I wonder if you will be here as long as I want you to.

I'm feeling like I'm falling for you and I don't really want to.

I didn't want this to happen.

How can you control feelings that were never really meant to be?

Will you be able to understand me?

Will you be able to take what my past had to offer me?

Are you wondering about a future with me?

Or are you just living in the moment?

I'm not sure where this is going.

Something is telling me to let this go because I don't want to hurt you.

And I definitely, don't want you to hurt me.

The more I'm around you, I want more of it.

Am I falling for you because I never meant for this to happen?

How can I let these feelings go?

When will this end because I don't like feeling this way since I have no control?

What will happen next time we are together?

Will there ever be a conversation about being together?

Will we just let whatever happen just happen?

What will this be?

You said you loved me

I remember you hit me, then you said you loved me.

I remember you choking me, then you said you loved me.

I remember you pulling out my hair, then you said you loved me.

I didn't leave because you told me you loved me.

Was I just naive, believing that you loved me?

Believing that's how love should be because you always told me you loved me?

Realization

Healing for someone else

I never knew that my guilt, humiliation and pain would bring me to this point.

I never knew that I would make it out.

It seemed like it would never end.

I didn't realize that that my pain would be somebody else's answered prayer.

I used to ask, "Why am I going through this and will it ever end"?

Now I know there was a simple reason.

To make me stronger in order to help someone else.

In order to use me.

In order to heal me.

Motivation From Within

I think I finally figured out how to express my feelings without being judged.

I can be me, without needing that nudge.

God is speaking to me, letting me know it will be okay.

I just hope it doesn't, just last a day.

I know I can do right.

I know I can do better.

God is saying is there anyway, I can let her.

As I listen, to what's good.

Its seems like something will always be bad.

I just don't want to be sad.

Feeling what I felt, when I was doing nothing, without a care in the world.

All I was thinking about was whether I wanted a boy or a girl.

I was blessed with everything I wanted in the world.

Yet, I'm still thinking about that baby girl.

Worn Feet Made Deaf Ears

I feel like the Lord is calling out to me, like this is my last chance.

There has been so many ups and downs.

So many obstacles.

I manage to make it out of them all.

I feel like there is one more obstacle to make it out of and I will be just fine.

I feel scared and afraid of the outcome.

I know God is still watching.

God already knows where I will end up.

Why am I so scared?

I've been through so much, that I just laugh and wonder how I made it through this long.

There is one last thing that I need to do to make God happy and make me feel at peace.

Maybe, I'm just too scared.

God already knows and is watching.

I can bear anything, I guess because I've already been through so much.

I feel like the Lord is calling out to me.

Until now

Until now, I know what it feels like to want someone.

Until now, I know what it feels like to have fun.

Until now, I know what it feels like to just be me.

Until now, I know what it feels like to just be free.

Until now, I understand how to make me happy.

Until now, I know how it feels to be alone.

Until now, I know where the pain comes from when I hear that sad song.

Until now, I know how to cope with my past.

Until now, I have the answers to what is being asked.

Until now, I know how to express how I feel.

Until now, I know that happiness is real.

Until now, I know how to let go.

Until now, I know just how to make things flow.

Until now, I know that the bad ends and good things begin.

Until now, I know that there's a beginning.

Until now, I know how it feels to have no feelings.

Until now, I know that I can be an inspiration.

Until now, I know how to handle the temptation.

Until now, I know where the pain came from.

Until now…

Future

Change

It's time for a change.

I hear this word so much but who actually cares?

Who cares about this and the future generation?

I'm not sure sometimes.

It has been determined that few people walk.

A lot of people talk.

Is this our own fault?

Should we change something that will only stop at the corner but will never turn?

Why are people so afraid to turn the corner?

Are they afraid of the outcome or what people will think?

Maybe they are only followers and not leaders.

Maybe they don't follow their own mind.

Only to go after others.

There is time for a change.

To build a better community, a better foundation and a better place to grow.

Who cares about our future?

Will we?

Will we just wait on the next person to turn the corner?

Watch them go around us as we just sit there?

How will we determine when the time is right?

When we run out of energy?

When no more time is left?

Will our great minds go to waste?

Who has time to think about that?

No one?

It's just time for a change.

Who will help?

Will you?

32 Strong

I am smiling because by the grace of God, I made it through my situations.

I am smiling because I could have been dead but God called someone to help me.

I am smiling because I could be without a car but by the grace of God, he provided me with a job.

I am smiling because by the grace of God he woke me up this morning.

I am smiling because by the grace of God he started me on my way to where I was headed today.

I am smiling because God brought someone into my life of whom I can talk to about my problems.

I am smiling because God watched over me while I was sleeping last night.

I am smiling because God helped me to pay my bills last week.

I am smiling because I am content with my current situation right now.

I am smiling because I am able to know why I am smiling.

I am smiling because I am able to write this down.

I am smiling because I am God's child.

I am smiling because God was able to forgive me for my sins.

I am smiling because I am loved by many.

I am smiling because I am blessed.

I am smiling because I know this is not the end.

Take me away

Take me away to that place.

That place where I always wanted to be.

That place that people rarely see.

I want to have no worries.

A place of peace.

Somewhere that I always wanted to be.

How can I get there?

Will I ever be able to make it there?

Where no one will care about how I look.

Where I wouldn't care what others thought of me.

I want to be in that place that people rarely see.

Happy and content every day because I'm where I always wanted to be.

Away from fear.

Away from drama.

Away from the heartache of life.

I'm not ready for what it has to offer.

Always tearing at me.

Then bring me back up again.

I'm so tired of this crazy rollercoaster.

I still want to just be somewhere that people rarely see.

No anger.

No sense of not belonging.

Nobody judging your thoughts.

No worries.

This is somewhere that I would love to be.

When will?

When will we learn to love again?

When will we learn to live off intuition again?

When will neighbors look after our kids again?

When will people stop following others?

When will we learn to be ourselves?

When will we all become equal?

When will we stop being greedy and wanting power?

When will we learn to love our community?

When will we learn to look after each other?

"I renew my spirit by releasing guilt, fear, and shame, acknowledging the truth and having accountability for my actions."

~Lisa Nichols

Sierra Dean has a passion for journaling her feelings and writing about knowledge that she has attained from her financial career. She started journaling as a way to express herself when she had a hard time expressing her emotions to other people. Sierra began to realize that journaling was therapeutic and healing in so many ways. She is the founder of Dean Diaries LLC, in which helps people to become authors along with creating journaling and writing templates to help people organize their thoughts. She has written for local newspapers, non-profits, financial firms and featured in the Huffington Post. As an author and freelance writer, Sierra knows how important it is for people to share knowledge.

For more information about Sierra Dean go to www.deandiaries.com

www.ingramcontent.com/pod-product-compliance
Lightning Source LLC
Chambersburg PA
CBHW021941040426
42448CB00008B/1184